PIANO | VOCAL | GUITAR • CD   **VOLUME 9**

PIANO PLAY-ALONG

CHILDREN'S SONGS

CONTENTS

ISBN 0-634-06909-8

HAL•LEONARD®
CORPORATION

7777 W. BLUEMOUND RD. P.O. BOX 13819 MILWAUKEE, WI 53213

Visit Hal Leonard Online at
www.halleonard.com

DO-RE-MI

from THE SOUND OF MUSIC

Lyrics by OSCAR HAMMERSTEIN II
Music by RICHARD RODGERS

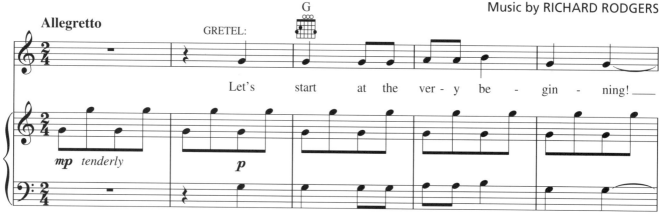

Let's start at the ver-y be-gin-ning! __

A ver-y good place to start, _____ When you

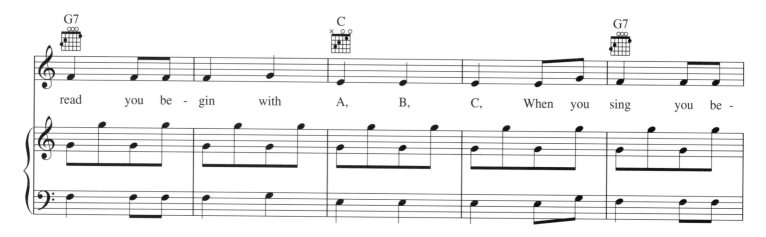

read you be-gin with A, B, C, When you sing you be-

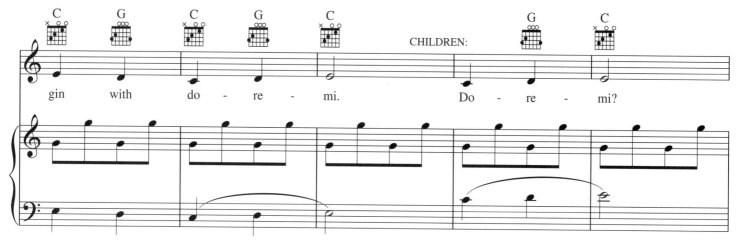

gin with do-re-mi. Do-re-mi?

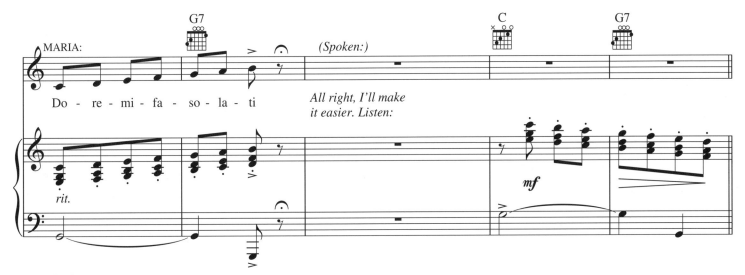

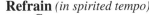

Refrain *(in spirited tempo)*

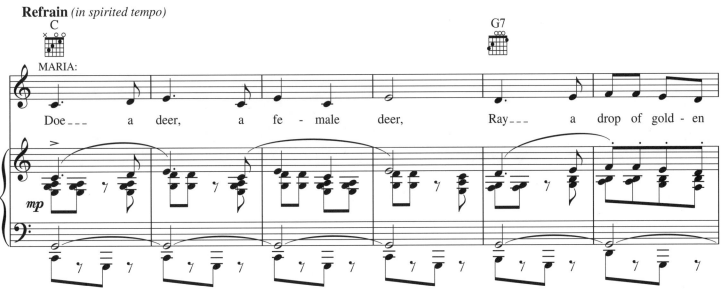

sun, _____ Me ___ a name I call my-self,

Far ___ a long, long way to run. _____ Sew ___ a nee-dle pull-ing

poco a poco cresc.

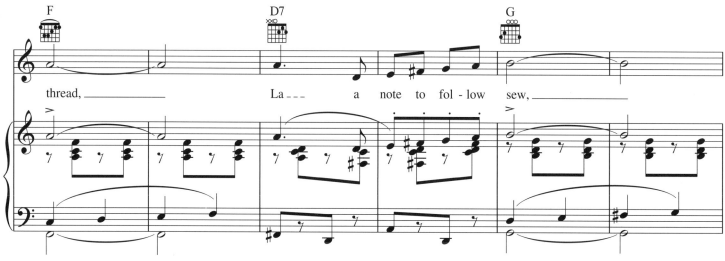

thread, _____ La ___ a note to fol-low sew, _____

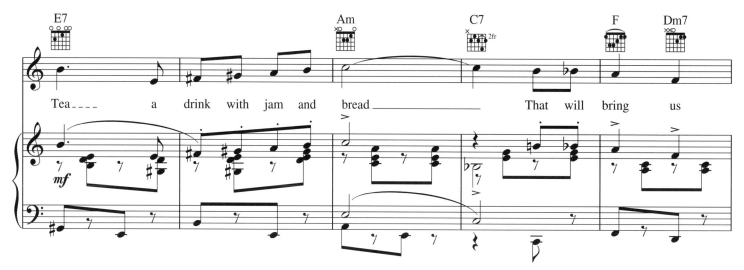

Tea ____ a drink with jam and bread _____ That will bring us

mf

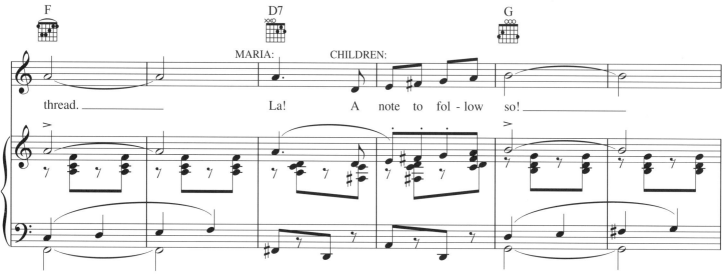

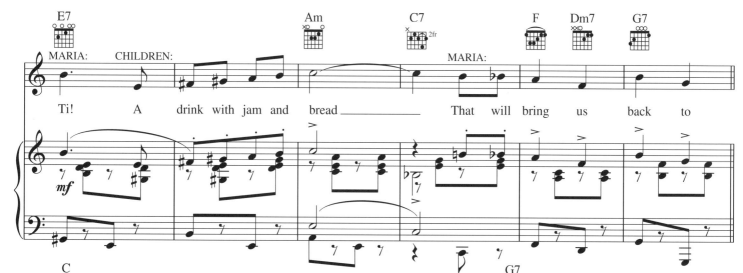

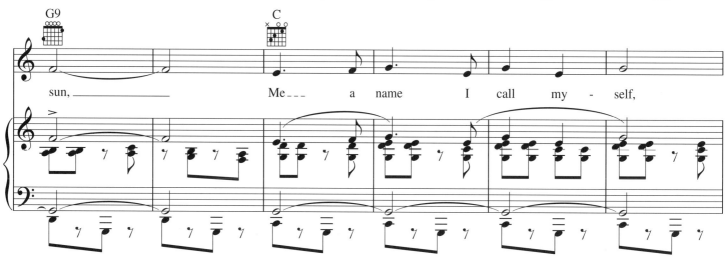

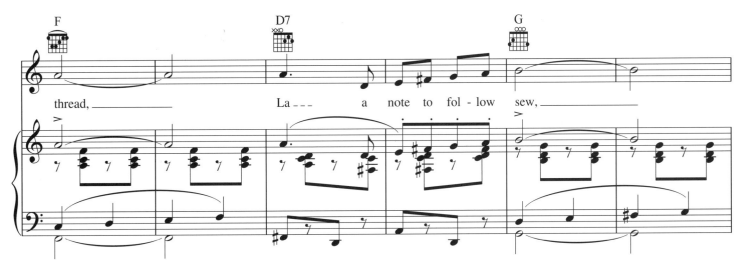

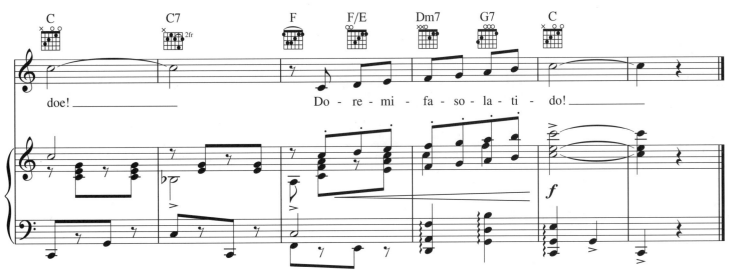

IT'S A SMALL WORLD

from "it's a small world" at Disneyland Park and Magic Kingdom Park

Words and Music by RICHARD M. SHERMAN
and ROBERT B. SHERMAN

March tempo

It's a world of laugh - ter, a world of
just one moon and one gold - en

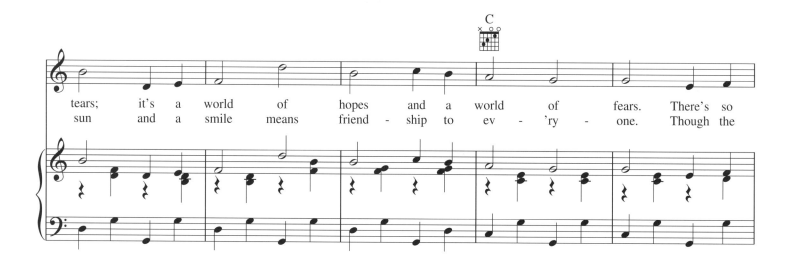

tears; it's a world of hopes and a world of fears. There's so
sun and a smile means friend - ship to ev - 'ry - one. Though the

much that we share that it's time we're a - ware, it's a
moun - tains di - vide and the o - ceans are wide, it's a

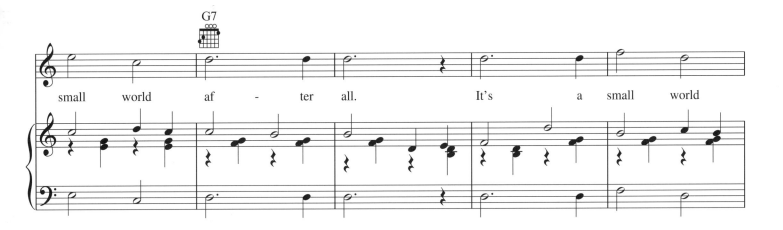

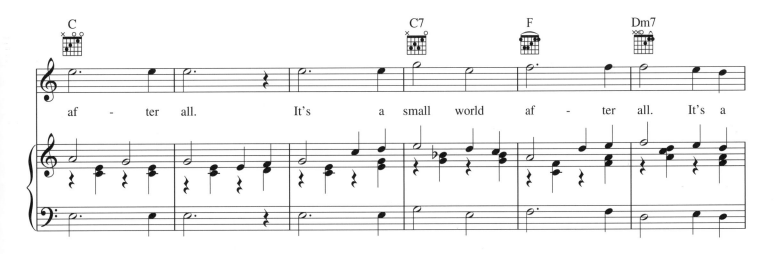

LINUS AND LUCY

By VINCE GUARALDI

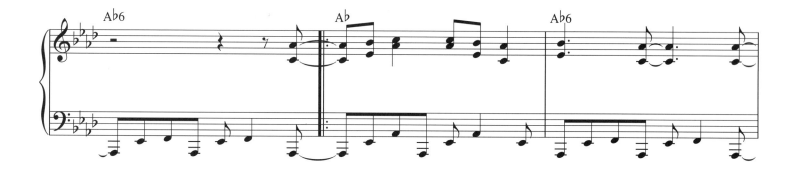

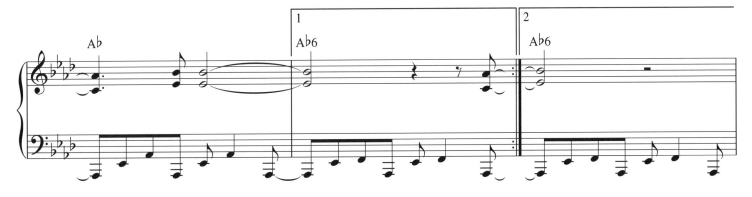

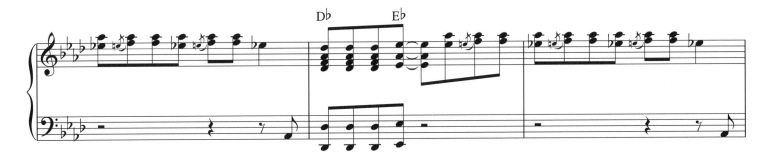

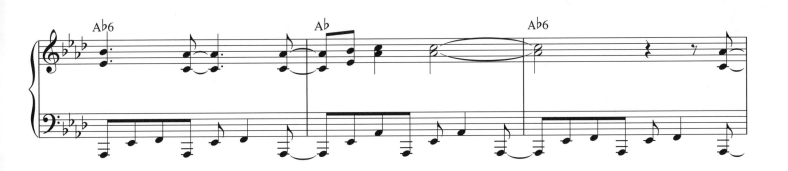

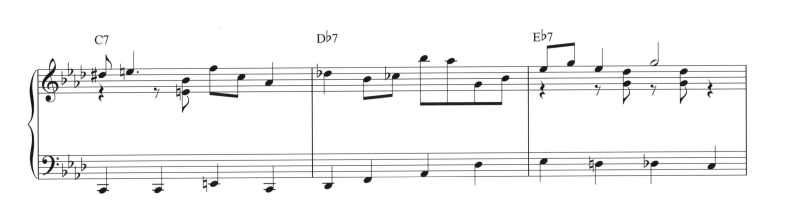

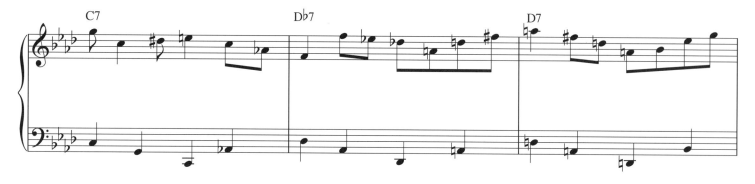

Original Tempo (♩♩ = ♩♩)

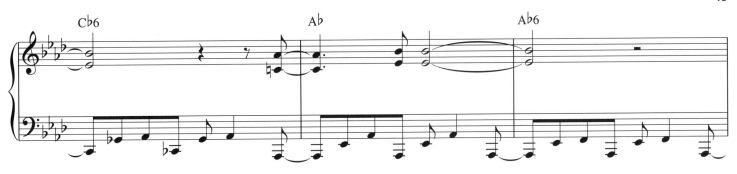

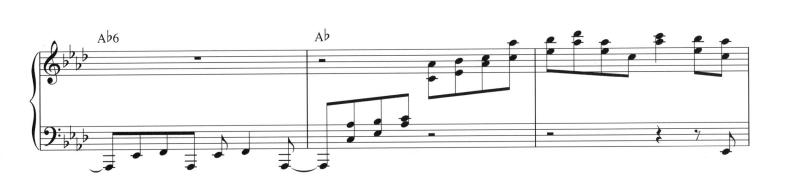

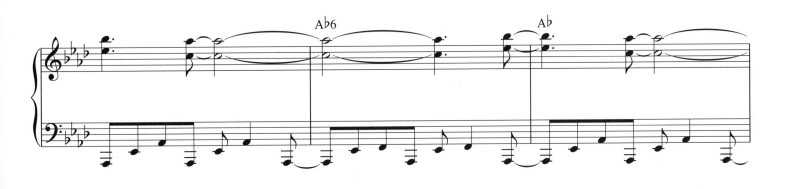

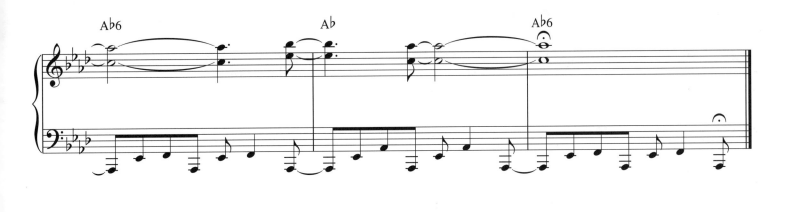

SESAME STREET THEME

Words by BRUCE HART,
JON STONE and JOE RAPOSO
Music by JOE RAPOSO

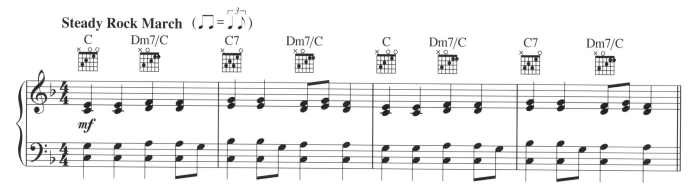

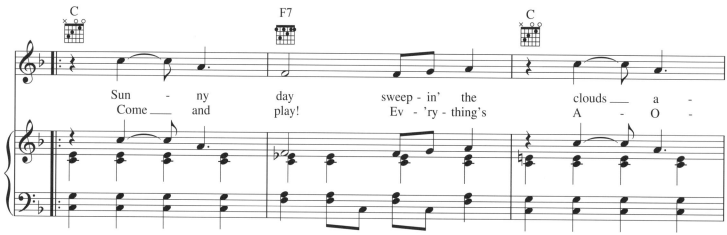

how to get to Ses - a - me Street? _____

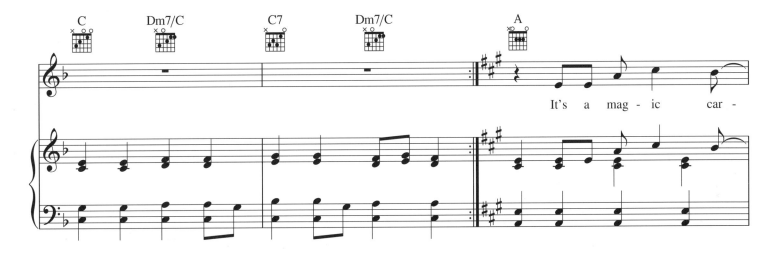

It's a mag - ic car -

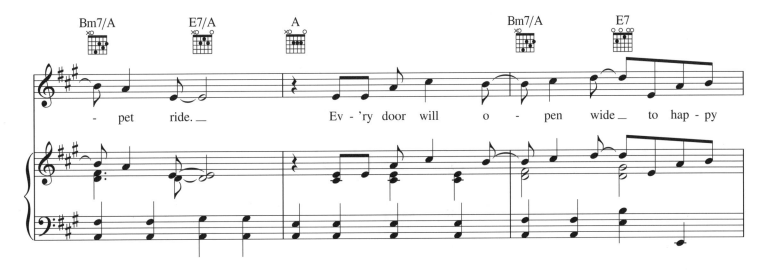

- pet ride. _ Ev - 'ry door will o - pen wide _ to hap - py

peo - ple like you. _ Hap - py peo - ple like... What a beau - ti - ful

sun - ny day sweep - in' the clouds ___ a -

way. On ___ my way to where the air is ___ sweet. ___

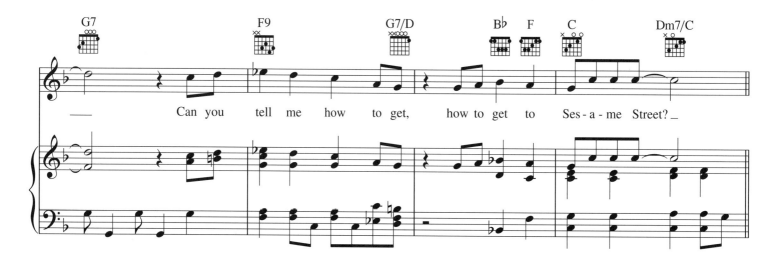

___ Can you tell me how to get, how to get to Ses - a - me Street? ___

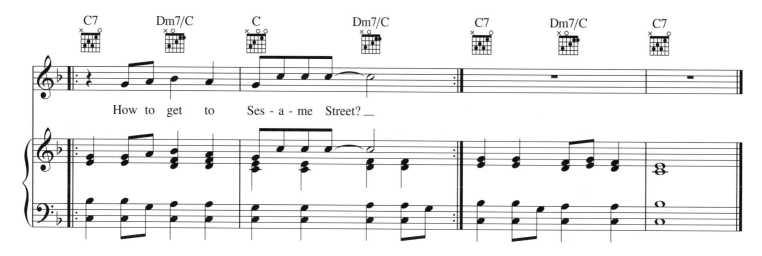

How to get to Ses - a - me Street? ___

WINNIE THE POOH

from Walt Disney's THE MANY ADVENTURES OF WINNIE THE POOH

Words and Music by RICHARD M. SHERMAN
and ROBERT B. SHERMAN

Moderate Waltz (♫ = ♫)

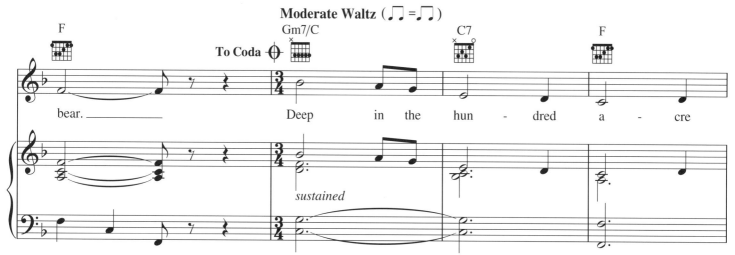

bear. _____ Deep in the hun - dred a - cre

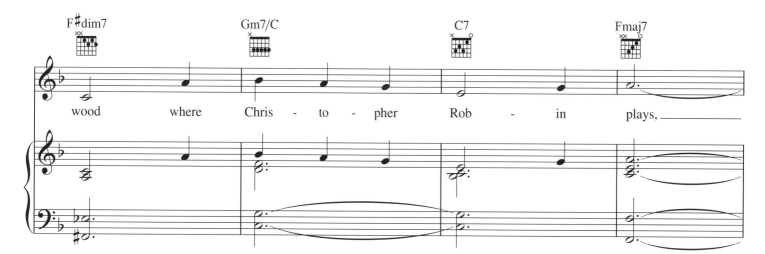

wood where Chris - to - pher Rob - in plays, _____

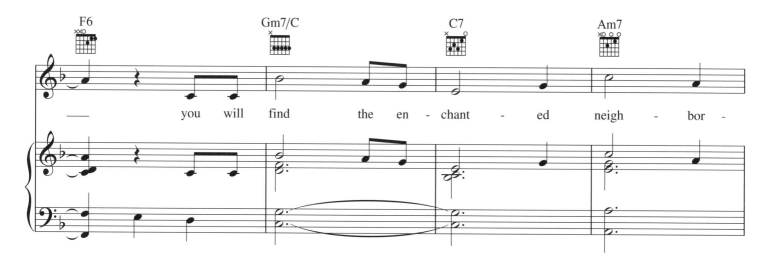

___ you will find the en - chant - ed neigh - bor -

hood of Chris - to - pher's child - hood days. _____

Tempo I (♩♩ = ♪♪³)

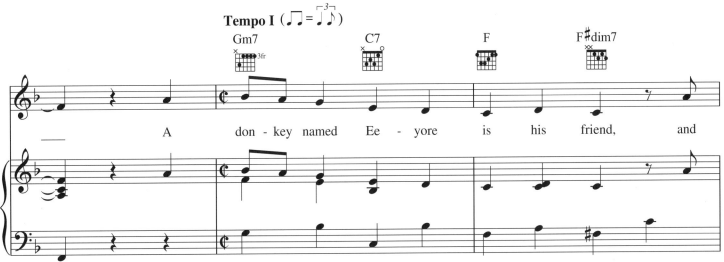

A don-key named Ee - yore is his friend, and

Kan - ga and lit - tle Roo. _____ There's Rab - bit and Pig - let

D.S. al Coda

and there's Owl but most of all Win - nie the Pooh.

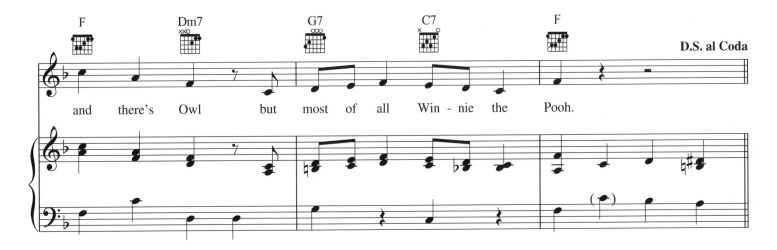

CODA

Wil - ly nil - ly sil - ly ole bear.

SING
from SESAME STREET

Words and Music by
JOE RAPOSO

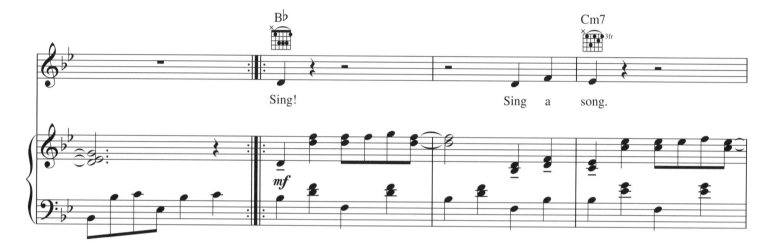

Sing! Sing a song.

Sing out loud, sing out strong.

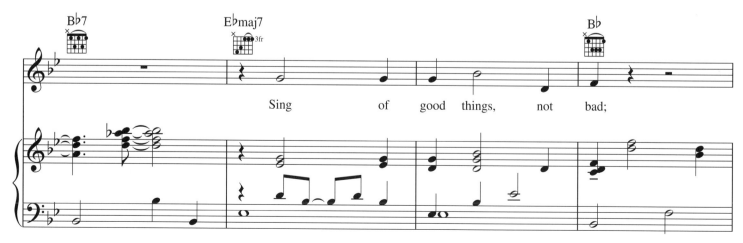

Sing of good things, not bad;

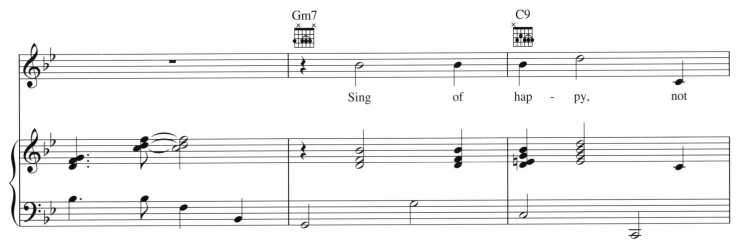

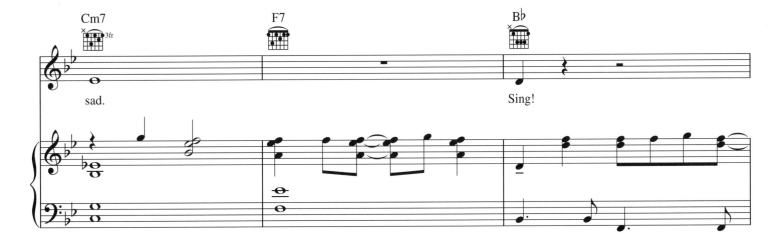

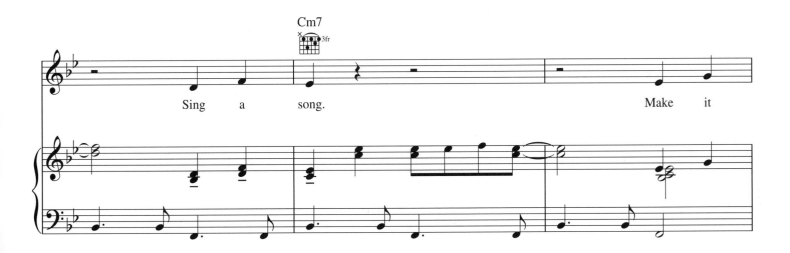

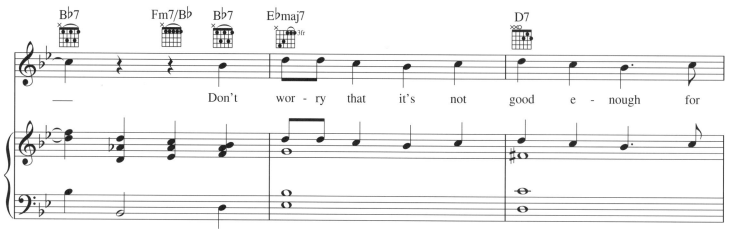

Don't wor-ry that it's not good e-nough for

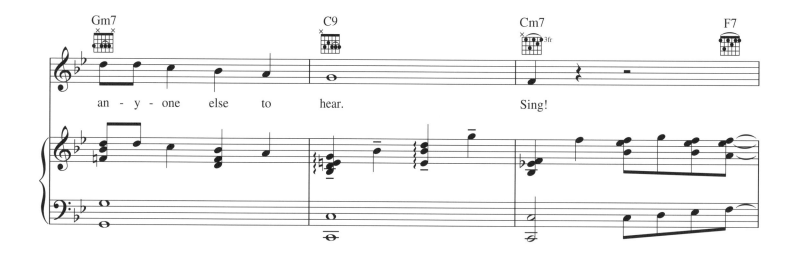

an-y-one else to hear. Sing!

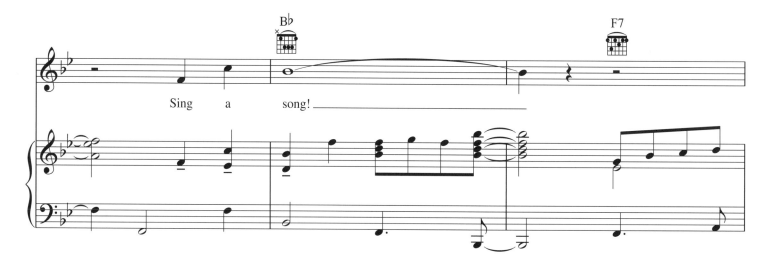

Sing a song! _____

La la do la da, La da la do la da, La da da la do la da. _

La do la da, La da la la da, Lo

da da la do la da.

La la do la da, La da la do la da, La da da la do la da.

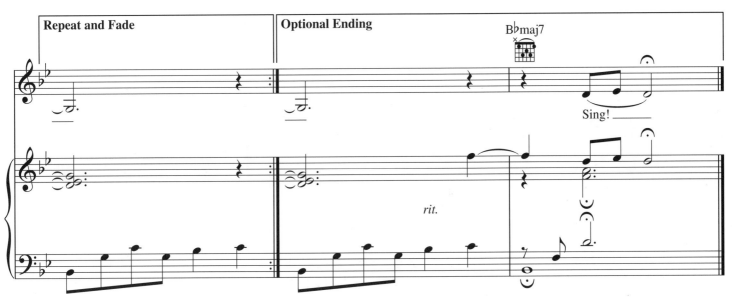

Repeat and Fade

Optional Ending

Sing!

rit.

WON'T YOU BE MY NEIGHBOR?

(It's a Beautiful Day in This Neighborhood)

from MISTER ROGERS' NEIGHBORHOOD

Words and Music by
FRED ROGERS

YELLOW SUBMARINE
from YELLOW SUBMARINE

Words and Music by JOHN LENNON
and PAUL McCARTNEY

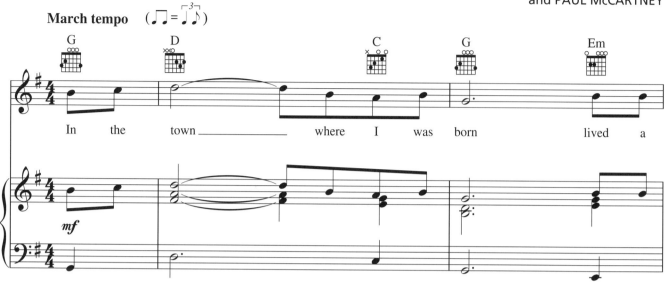

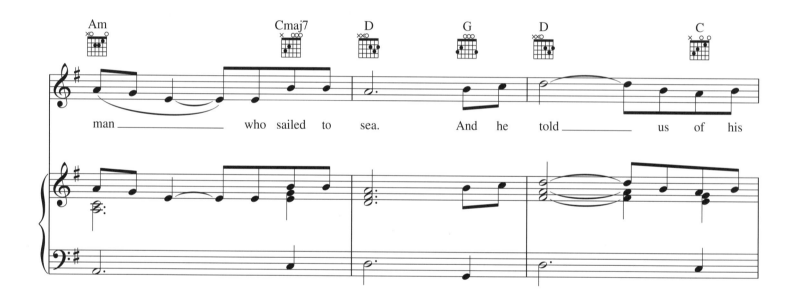

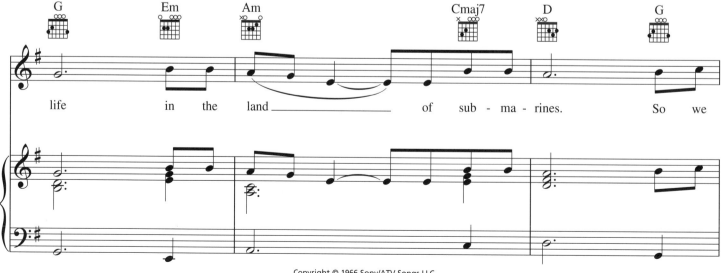

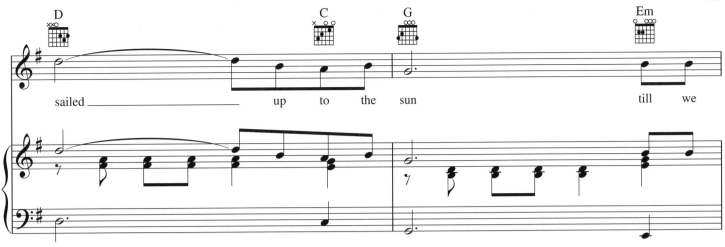

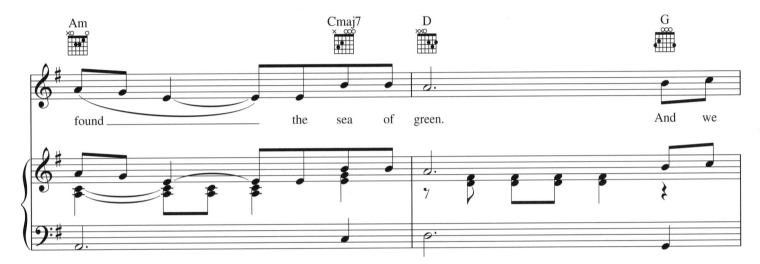

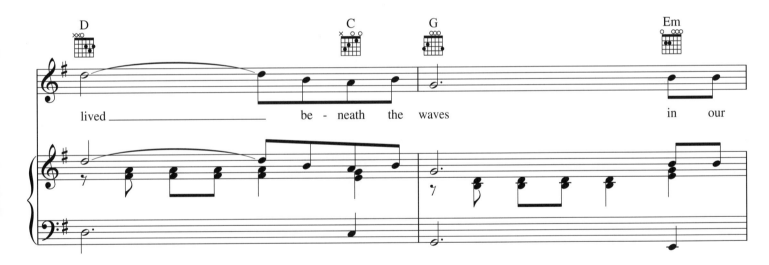

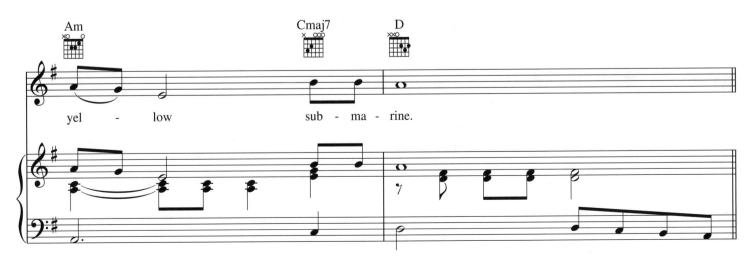

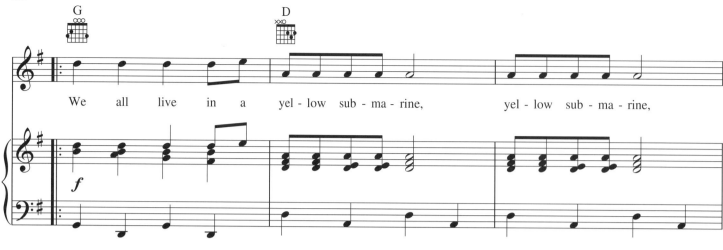

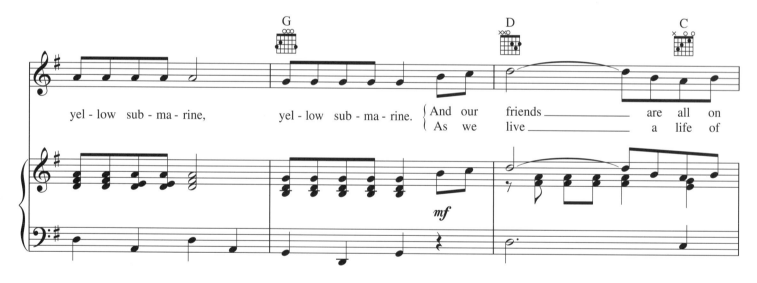

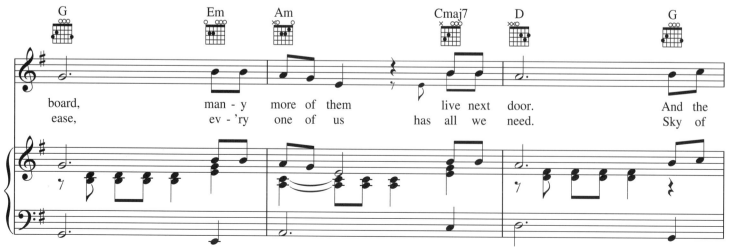

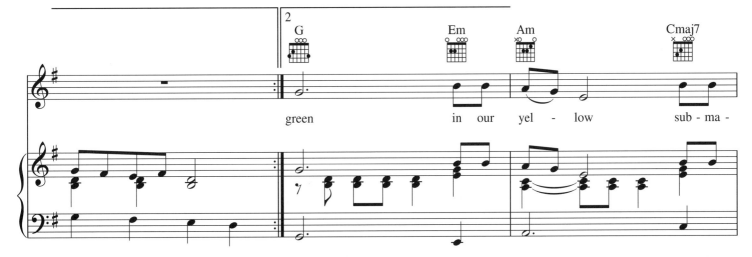

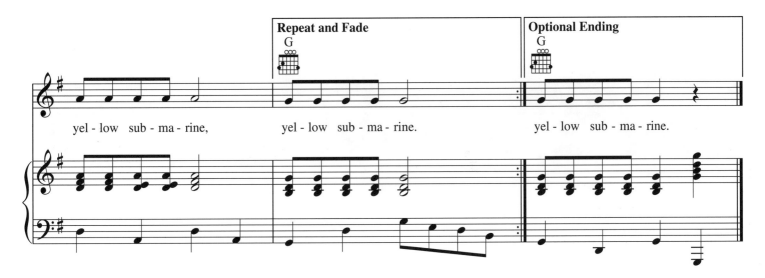

THE ULTIMATE SONGBOOKS

 HAL•LEONARD

PIANO PLAY-ALONG

These great songbook/CD packs come with our standard arrangements for piano and voice with guitar chord frames plus a CD. The CD includes a full performance of each song, as well as a second track without the piano part so you can play "lead" with the band!

VOLUME 1
MOVIE MUSIC
Come What May • Forrest Gump – Main Title (Feather Theme) • My Heart Will Go On (Love Theme from *Titanic*) • The Rainbow Connection • Tears in Heaven • A Time for Us • Up Where We Belong • Where Do I Begin (Love Theme).
00311072 P/V/G.....................$12.95

VOLUME 2
JAZZ BALLADS
Autumn in New York • Do You Know What It Means to Miss New Orleans • Georgia on My Mind • In a Sentimental Mood • More Than You Know • The Nearness of You • The Very Thought of You • When Sunny Gets Blue.
00311073 P/V/G.....................$12.95

VOLUME 3
TIMELESS POP
Ebony and Ivory • Every Breath You Take • From a Distance • I Write the Songs • In My Room • Let It Be • Oh, Pretty Woman • We've Only Just Begun.
00311074 P/V/G.....................$12.95

VOLUME 4
BROADWAY CLASSICS
Ain't Misbehavin' • Cabaret • If I Were a Bell • Memory • Oklahoma • Some Enchanted Evening • The Sound of Music • You'll Never Walk Alone.
00311075 P/V/G.....................$12.95

VOLUME 5
DISNEY
Beauty and the Beast • Can You Feel the Love Tonight • Colors of the Wind • Go the Distance • Look Through My Eyes • A Whole New World • You'll Be in My Heart • You've Got a Friend in Me.
00311076 P/V/G.....................$12.95

VOLUME 6
COUNTRY STANDARDS
Blue Eyes Crying in the Rain • Crazy • King of the Road • Oh, Lonesome Me • Ring of Fire • Tennessee Waltz • You Are My Sunshine • Your Cheatin' Heart.
00311077 P/V/G.....................$12.95

VOLUME 7
LOVE SONGS
Can't Help Falling in Love • (They Long to Be) Close to You • Here, There and Everywhere • How Deep Is Your Love • I Honestly Love You • Maybe I'm Amazed • Wonderful Tonight • You Are So Beautiful.
00311078 P/V/G.....................$12.95

VOLUME 8
CLASSICAL THEMES
Can Can • Habanera • Humoresque • In the Hall of the Mountain King • Minuet in G Major • Piano Concerto No. 21 in C Major ("Elvira Madigan"), Second Movement Excerpt • Prelude in E Minor, Op. 28, No. 4 • Symphony No. 5 in C Minor, First Movement Excerpt.
00311079 Piano Solo $12.95

VOLUME 9
CHILDREN'S SONGS
Do-Re-Mi • It's a Small World • Linus and Lucy • Sesame Street Theme • Sing • Winnie the Pooh • Won't You Be My Neighbor? (It's a Beautiful Day in This Neighborhood) • Yellow Submarine.
0311080 P/V/G $12.95

VOLUME 10
WEDDING CLASSICS
Air on the G String • Ave Maria • Bridal Chorus • Canon in D • Jesu, Joy of Man's Desiring • Ode to Joy • Trumpet Voluntary • Wedding March.
00311081 Piano Solo................$12.95

VOLUME 11
WEDDING FAVORITES
All I Ask of You • Don't Know Much • Endless Love • Grow Old with Me • In My Life • Longer • Wedding Processional • You and I.
00311097 P/V/G $12.95

VOLUME 12
CHRISTMAS FAVORITES
Blue Christmas • The Christmas Song (Chestnuts Roasting on an Open Fire) • Do You Hear What I Hear • Here Comes Santa Claus (Right down Santa Claus Lane) • I Saw Mommy Kissing Santa Claus • Let It Snow! Let It Snow! Let It Snow! • Merry Christmas, Darling • Silver Bells.
00311137 P/V/G $12.95

VOLUME 13
YULETIDE FAVORITES
Angels We Have Heard on High • Away in a Manger • Deck the Hall • The First Noel • Go, Tell It on the Mountain • Jingle Bells • Joy to the World • O Little Town of Bethlehem.
00311138 P/V/G.....................$12.95

VOLUME 14
POP BALLADS
Have I Told You Lately • I'll Be There for You • It's All Coming Back to Me Now • Looks Like We Made It • Rainy Days and Monday • Say You, Say Me • She's Got a Way • Your Song.
00311145 P/V/G.....................$12.95

VOLUME 15
FAVORITE STANDARDS
Call Me • The Girl from Ipanema (Garota De Ipanema) • Moon River • My Way • Satin Doll • Smoke Gets in Your Eyes • Strangers in the Night • The Way You Look Tonight.
00311146 P/V/G.....................$12.95

VOLUME 16
TV CLASSICS
The Brady Bunch • Green Acres Theme • Happy Days • Johnny's Theme • Love Boat Theme • Mister Ed • The Munsters Theme • Where Everybody Knows Your Name.
00311147 P/V/G.....................$12.95

VOLUME 17
MOVIE FAVORITES
Back to the Future • Theme from E.T. (The Extra-Terrestrial) • Footloose • For All We Know • Somewhere in Time • Somewhere Out There • Theme from *Terms of Endearment* • You Light Up My Life.
00311148 P/V/G.....................$12.95

VOLUME 18
JAZZ STANDARDS
All the Things You Are • Bluesette • Easy Living • I'll Remember April • Isn't It Romantic? • Stella by Starlight • Tangerine • Yesterdays.
00311149 P/V/G.....................$12.95

VOLUME 19
CONTEMPORARY HITS
Beautiful • Calling All Angels • Don't Know Why • If I Ain't Got You • 100 Years • This Love • A Thousand Miles • You Raise Me Up.
00311162 P/V/G.....................$12.95

VOLUME 20
R&B BALLADS
After the Love Has Gone • All in Love Is Fair • Hello • I'll Be There • Let's Stay Together • Midnight Train to Georgia • Tell It like It Is • Three Times a Lady.
00311163 P/V/G.....................$12.95

VOLUME 21
BIG BANDS
All or Nothing at All • Apple Honey • April in Paris • Cherokee (Indian Love Song) • In the Mood • Opus One • Stardust • Stompin' at the Savoy.
00311164 P/V/G.....................$12.95

VOLUME 22
ROCK CLASSICS
Against All Odds (Take a Look at Me Now) • Bennie and the Jets • Come Sail Away • Do It Again • Free Bird • Jump • Wanted Dead or Alive • We Are the Champions.
00311165 P/V/G.....................$12.95

VOLUME 23
WORSHIP CLASSICS
Awesome God • How Majestic Is Your Name • Lord, Be Glorified • Lord, I Lift Your Name on High • Praise the Name of Jesus • Shine, Jesus, Shine • Step by Step • There Is a Redeemer.
00311166 P/V/G.....................$12.95

VOLUME 24
LES MISÉRABLES
Bring Him Home • Castle on a Cloud • Do You Hear the People Sing? • Drink with Me (To Days Gone By) • Empty Chairs at Empty Tables • I Dreamed a Dream • A Little Fall of Rain • On My Own.
00311169 P/V/G.....................$12.95

VOLUME 26
ANDREW LLOYD WEBBER FAVORITES
All I Ask of You • Amigos Para Siempre (Friends for Life) • As If We Never Said Goodbye • Everything's Alright • Memory • No Matter What • Tell Me on a Sunday • You Must Love Me.
00311178 P/V/G.....................$12.95

VOLUME 27
ANDREW LLOYD WEBBER GREATS
Any Dream Will Do • Don't Cry for Me Argentina • I Don't Know How to Love Him • The Music of the Night • The Phantom of the Opera • Unexpected Song • Whistle Down the Wind • With One Look.
00311179 P/V/G.....................$12.95

Disney characters and artwork © Disney Enterprises, Inc.

FOR MORE INFORMATION, SEE YOUR LOCAL MUSIC DEALER, OR WRITE TO:

HAL•LEONARD® CORPORATION
7777 W. BLUEMOUND RD. P.O. BOX 13819 MILWAUKEE, WI 53213

Visit Hal Leonard Online at **www.halleonard.com**